D0435625

POCKET PAINTERS

VAN GOGH

1853 – 1890

CLARKSON POTTER/PUBLISHERS

NEW YORK

Van Gogh

Vincent van Gogh (1853-1890) only found his true vocation in 1880, a mere ten years before his death, but he brought to his study of painting the same fervour that he had shown as a lay preacher. At the end of five years of hard and largely self-taught apprenticeship in Holland, during which he struggled with technique – and with the poverty that he would never shake off – he achieved some mastery of oils in a series of assured if sombre paintings of peasant life.

In 1886, at the suggestion of his brother Theo, he came to Paris where he met some of the Impressionists, broadened the scope of his subject-matter, lightened his palette and experimented briefly with the techniques of the pointillists and Japanese printmakers.

When, oppressed by city life, Vincent headed off to Provence in 1888 with the dream of setting up an artists' colony there, he told Theo that he wanted to paint like a Japanese artist. The dream was shattered when a three-month visit by Gauguin ended disastrously with Vincent's first breakdown, but he painted more and more like a man possessed: portraits, still-lifes, interiors, self-portraits and, above all, the drama of the landscape. In a feverish adaptation of the pointillists' technique he laid his colours out in ribbons, sometimes even squeezing it straight from the tube on to the canvas in his hurry to express his burning vision of nature and its magic, in which the tortured cypresses and dazzling sunflowers began to seem like sacred motifs.

Tormented by hallucinations as well as sheer loneliness, Vincent admitted himself to the mental hospital at St Rémy, where for a year he found some relief and was able to paint intermittently with increasing power. In May 1890, however, he discharged himself and returned north. He seemed to have found tranquillity under the care of Dr Gachet at Auvers, although the paintings of this brief period suggest otherwise. On 27 July, in the grip of despair, he shot himself, and died two days later.

Heartbreaking as the story of this passionate misfit is, his immortality at least is assured. It is a sobering thought that, had his struggle ended a mere two years earlier, before he moved to Arles and there, supported from afar by the love, encouragement and financial help of his admirable brother, gloriously fulfilled himself as a painter, he would now be regarded as a sad peripheral figure, and not as the tragic giant of nineteenth-century art. ◼

*Landscape in
Brabant*

Oil on canvas
1885
22 × 37 cm

This early landscape, probably painted
at Nuenen, is far removed from the
bold, passionate canvasses of the Arles
period. Nevertheless the gloomy
atmosphere of the drab terrain is
effectively conveyed.

The Weaver

Oil on canvas
1884
37 × 45 cm

Vincent's spell as a lay missionary in Belgian mining communities had made him highly sympathetic to the labouring classes. The weaver, surrounded by his apparatus, made him think of *'prisoners in I know not what horrible cage'*.

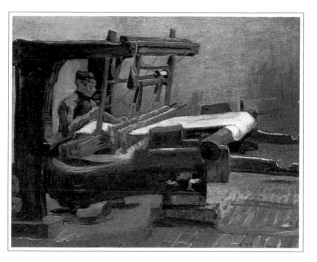

***Peasant Woman
from Nuenen***

Oil on canvas
1885
45 × 27 cm

Left – During his Dutch period Vincent found most of his subject-matter in the lives of peasants, whom he painted with grave dignity. Their back-breaking work in the fields would remain a compelling theme until the end of his life.

Overleaf – The subject of this early drawing, one of a series depicting the four seasons, appealed strongly to Vincent as an allegorical symbol of renewal. He would return to it in his St Rémy period in his reworking of Millet's painting.

The Sower

Pencil and pen
1884
6 × 14 cm

Fishing in the Spring

Oil on canvas
1887
49 × 58 cm

Early in 1886 Vincent arrived in Paris, where for two years he was bombarded with new ideas and experiences – chiefly, though his friendship with painters such as Paul Signac, the revelation of neo-Impressionist ideas about colour and light. Here he is experimenting with dabs of paint.

Restaurant de la Sirène at Asnières

Oil on canvas
1887
57 × 68 cm

Vincent spent most of June 1887 painting with Emile Bernard at Asnières, on the Ile de la Grande Jatte, then a popular resort for the boisterous boating crowd.

A Wheatfield
with a Lark

Oil on canvas
1887
54 × 64.5 cm

This animated canvas from the Paris
period, with its golden stubble,
swaying corn and agitated sky, seems
strangely prophetic of the style and the
storms to come when Vincent moved
to Provence.

Sunflowers

Oil on canvas
1887
43 × 61 cm

The sight of sunflowers in a Parisian
window struck Vincent so forcibly that
they became an obsession – and his
most popular and distinctive subject.
He painted them many times, racing to
complete each canvas in one sitting
before the flowers wilted.

Pollard Willows and Setting Sun

Oil on canvas
1888
31 × 34 cm

Paris had opened Vincent's eyes to colour, but now he wanted more of it – pure colour – and in Provence he found it. *The pale orange of the sunsets makes the fields appear blue,'* he exclaimed in a letter to Emile Bernard from Arles. *'The sun is a splendid yellow.'*

**The Promenade
of the Alyscamps**

Oil on canvas
1888
92 × 73.5 cm

At Arles, Vincent found a compelling,
if untypical subject in the site of a vast
Roman burial ground, of which this
avenue is virtually all that remains.
Vincent was struck by the atmosphere
of the place and painted it several
times.

**Sunday Evening
at Arles**

Oil on canvas
1888
74 × 91 cm

The harsh, brilliant colours of the
south had an overwhelming effect on
Vincent, who described himself as
working in a frenzy. The result was an
intensity of colour, such as this yellow,
that had never been painted before.

La Mousmé

Oil on canvas
1888
74 × 60 cm

After a few months of painting the
Provençal landscape, Vincent began to
find time for portraits. The title of this
charming study of youth is a Japanese
word meaning young girl, which he
borrowed from a Pierre Loti novel.

Sunflowers

Oil on canvas
1888
91 × 72 cm

In August 1888 Vincent began what was to become a sublime series of paintings of his beloved sunflowers, with which he planned to decorate his studio. *I am hard at it,* he wrote to Theo, *'painting with the enthusiasm of a Marseillais eating bouillabaisse.'*

Overleaf – A night sky such as this had already been described in a letter to Theo: *'In the blue depth the stars were sparkling, greenish, yellow, white, rose, brighter, flashing more like jewels, than they do at home – even in Paris: opals you might call them, emeralds, lapis, rubies, sapphires.'*

**The Dance Hall
at Arles**

Oil on canvas
1888
65 × 78.5 cm

The dazzling yellow of sunflowers and
the fierce Provençal sun is the hallmark
of Vincent's Arles period. Even this
indoor scene is dominated by flat areas
of yellow, perhaps influenced by
Gauguin, whose ill-fated collaboration
was to be the only one at Vincent's
'studio of the south'.

Portrait of Dr Rey

Oil on canvas
1889
64 × 53 cm

When Vincent was admitted to the
hospital at Arles following his
breakdown he was lucky to be under
the supervision of Dr Félix Rey, who
not only showed him kindness but
recognized his genius. Friends of the
young doctor who saw this
sympathetic protrait many years later
said that it was a very good likeness.

*St Paul's Hospital,
St Rémy*

Oil on canvas
1889
63 × 48 cm

During his time as a mental patient at
St Rémy, Vincent suffered attacks
which lasted for a week or more. When
he was able to paint, his work would be
frenzied or relatively calm, according
to his state of mind.

***The Prison
Court-Yard***

Oil on canvas
1890
80 × 64 cm

At the St Rémy asylum Vincent
sometimes set himself the instructive
and, for him, consoling task of copying
works by painters he admired, such as
the *Pieta* by Delacroix. The choice of
Gustave Doré's drawing of the exercise
yard at Newgate Prison had an
altogether grimmer symbolism.

The Church at Auvers

Oil on canvas
1890
94 × 74 cm

Although Vincent described the content of the painting in measured terms in a letter to Theo, its deformed lines are strongly suggestive of mental turmoil. Whatever the final straw was that drove him to suicide, he died believing himself to be a burden to others and failure as an artist.

Published by Clarkson N. Potter, Inc., 201 East 50th Street,
New York, New York 10022. Member of the Crown Publishing Group.

Random House, Inc. New York, Toronto, London, Sydney, Auckland.

CLARKSON N. POTTER, POTTER, and colophon are
trademarks of Clarkson N. Potter, Inc.

Originally published in Great Britain by Pavilion Books Limited in 1994

Manufactured in Italy

ISBN 0-517-59968-6

10   9   8   7   6   5   4   3   2   1

First American Edition

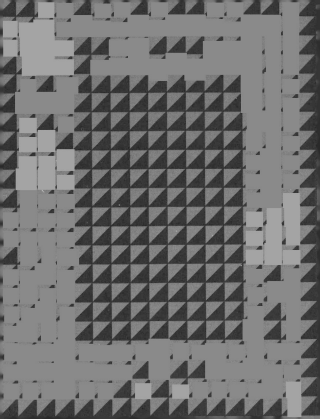